Y0-BWE-530

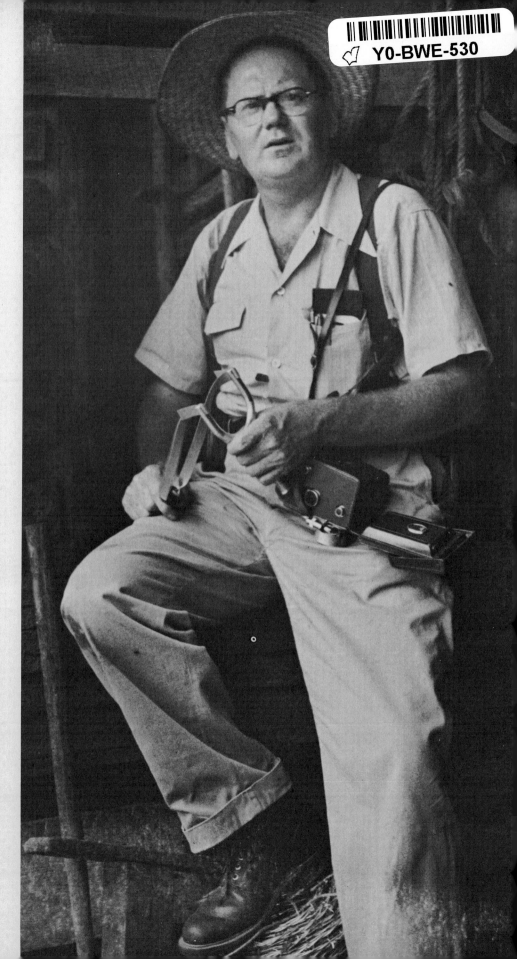

My Friend, Joe Clark . . .

One definition of a sophisticated man is a person who is entirely at home in his surroundings, no matter what they are and by that standard Joe Clark is the most sophisticated man I know. The Hill Billy Snap Shooter is equally at ease in the plush palace of an automobile baron or pitching pebbles into the scrawny brook that trickles through his farm near Cumberland Gap, Tenn. In an earlier book about Detroit, Joe captured the warmth and excitement of his adopted city. But to Joe, Tennessee is still "down home"—a place brimming with friends and family, the pride of owning land, and memories of a boyhood well wasted. On these pages Joe sings a paean to his home country. It is a book not about Tennessee, but Joe Clark's Tennessee—and that is something special.

Tom Flaherty
Associate Editor
Life Magazine

Privately printed for the Tennessee Squire Association

Copyright 1965 By The Tennessee Squire Association

Printed in the United States of America by

Kingsport Press, Inc., Kingsport, Tennessee

BACK HOME
BY JOE CLARK HBSS

LESSONS

Nature's simple secrets
   Can hide in quiet pools
And Life's greatest lessons
   Are not all learned in schools.

THE ROW YOU HOE

The patterns of life
  Are finely drawn
Like harvest fields
  So neatly sown.

Here a thistle
  And there a weed
Will sprout among
  The planted seed.

And where you'd point
  With bated pride
Will grow a thorn
  Deep in your side.

But you must hoe
  And pull the weeds
And cultivate
  With kindly deeds.

And care each day
  For tender shoots
And fertilize
  The hungry roots.

And tend your crop
  That it shall grow
Keeping straight
  The row you hoe.

There's one thing more
  You ought to know
You cannot reap
  Before you sow.

HIDEBOUND

There ain't much to learn
    And little to do
If you're hidebound
    And pigheaded, too.

MAN

Man is a fragile hunk of mud,
He's made of muscle, bone and blood;
There ain't much hair upon his head
It grows upon his face instead.

He has a brain that in the main
Must strain to keep him from the rain;
His will is weak and very small
So he grows fat instead of tall.

He's mostly short of money, too,
In spite of all that he can do;
Yet, if he's rich with lots of hay
He can only eat three meals a day.

Though he succeed in life as such
He won't enjoy it very much;
He's prone to sweat and boil and stew
About the things he cannot do;

About the times he didn't bet,
About the raise he didn't get,
About the debts he hasn't paid,
About the million he hasn't made.

All in all he's a weakly cuss,
And hardly worth a little fuss;
Yet, man is strong and if he tries
He'll surely live until he dies.

HOMESICK

Pretty soon I'm going to be'
Way down yonder in Tennessee,
I'm going back again to climb
Those old, old hills I left behind.

Pretty soon you're going to see
Somebody looking just like me
Swinging across the mountain high
With a homebound look in his eye.

Pretty soon I'm going to dine
At Ma's table rich and fine
On hominy grits and brandywine
And Southern fried that's mighty fine.

THE LAND BEYOND

When I was a lad I stood in a valley
In a valley deep and wide
And I looked up at a hill,
A hill that was so rugged
And so steep and high,
I stood and I looked and I wondered
As lads so often do
Why the hill was so rugged
And so steep and high
But most of all I wondered
What was on the other side.

Now I've grown to be a man,
Tall and strong and wise,
And many the sights I've seen
Under the wandering skies,
Yet, when I stand in a valley
A valley deep and wide
And I look at a hill I wonder
What is on the other side.

TOMORROW

Up and down the dusty road
  Up and down the valley
Up and down the highway
  To see my pretty Sally.

Up and down the blackgum tree
  Up and down the hollow
Up and down the mountain,
  I'll see her tomorrow.

NO REGRETS

The river runs on
Old times are gone,
New things come in
What's been has been.

RELAX

When worry and fret come your way
About the bills you have to pay,

The many things you have to do
Nothing ever goes right with you.

Can't pay the rent or buy no shoes,
You flounder in them worry blues

It's better then to just relax
And spare your feeble mind the tax,

It's rather vain to strain your brain
When thinkin' goes against the grain,

So hang your hat upon the rack
And lean your chair against the shack,

Just put a million in the bank
And leave your mind
    completely blank.

THE GOOD OLD DAYS

give me back the good old days
     The days I used to know
'hen simple things were modern things,
     The pace was pleasant and slow.

 house uncluttered with plumbing
     A well out in the yard
 n axe for chopping firewood with
     And make my muscles hard.

 he general store for loafing
     Or a first class checker game
 box of ashes for spitting
     And never hitting same.

 ut most of all from those grand days
     So packed with memories
 ve me a house way down the path
     Where I can sit and freeze.

IN LONESOME TENNESSEE

Down yonder in the valley
   In lonesome Tennessee
Sits my little Sally
   A waitin' there for me.

Down yonder in the valley
   Oh how I long to be
A sittin' by my Sally
   In lonesome Tennessee.

SCHOOL DAYS

Oh, the hardness of the benches
   And the hardness of my head
And the hardness of the lessons
   Was an awful thing to dread.

LONG AGO

There was a little white school
   On the side of a hill
And a pretty little girl
   That I remember still.

A BOY'S DREAMS

A barefoot lad
  He roams the hills
And dreams of land
  Where fortune fills
The hopes of one
  Who toils and tills.

In dreams he sails
  The oceans wide
Through storm and gale
  And friendly tide,
When duty calls
  He does not hide.

And in his dreams
  This little man
Builds a future
  As boyhood can
For a boy's dreams
  Become the man.

GERMS

We didn't fight germs
when I was a kid.
We ettem.
Alive.

I PLEDGE

To loaf along Life's highways
     To feel its shifting sands
Climb its hills, view its valleys
     And see its verdant lands.

To feast on bountiful harvests
     That grow along its ways
To watch the glowing sunsets
     That end its shining days.

To greet each morning joyously,
     To sing the livelong day,
To laugh with happy comrades,
     To while this life away.

THINGS I'D LIKE TO DO AGAIN

To build a dam across a brook
　　To wade and fish in quiet streams
To climb a hill to take a look
　　To revel in boyhood dreams.

To leap from out the loft so high
　　To explore the barn and fields
To roam o'er the hills and dells
　　To enjoy what nature yields.

To pick the wild grapes from the vine
　　To find the blackberries ripe
To taste the pawpaws wild and sweet
　　To explore my manly might.

To romp and roam with dog and gun
　　Through forest, dale and glen
To breathe the free and open air
　　And to walk with nature's kin.

MOLASSES MAKING TIME

'Lasses making time
Was a happy time
With lots of work to be done
But the end of day
Brought its mirth and play
With a host of girls and fun.

EDUCATION

To read, rite and cipher
    Proves you've been to school,
A fine engraved diploma
    Proves you ain't no fool.

You've got a education
    You're learned and you're wise
And a fine reputation
    For the way you dot your eyes.

You are a educated man,
    Of letters and of ink;
One question may I ask
    When will you learn to think?

BACK YONDER

If you lived in the country
    On a Saturday night
It was clean all the lamps
    To make the world bright.

GREEN WAS THE MEADOW

Green was the meadow
  Tall was the corn
High was the mountain
  Where I was born.

Fair was the valley
  Warm was the sun
And clear was the stream
  Where I was born.

Sweet is the memory,
  Pleasant the days . . .
Of boyhood wanderings
  Of boyhood ways.

SPRING THOUGHTS

When earth is soft and pleasant
    To touch of tiller's hand
And crops are being planted
    All across the land.

When the mule is being prodded,
    The sun is climbing high
And work's to be accomplished,
    Time is passing by.

When hopes are swiftly rising
    To soar into the sky
For all the crops we'll harvest
    In the by and by.

When the sap is swiftly rising,
    The breeze begins to warm
And the birds sing in the spring
    Down yonder on the farm.

When lovers walk together
    In twilight's mellow glow
And whisper to each other
    Of things they aim to grow.

Then it's great to be alive,
    To breathe the wholesome air,
To have someone to love you,
    To be in love with her.

It's never too cold to chop wood
when you're out of fire.

MOONSHINE

There's an Indiana moon
  Or so it seems to me
Because the crooners croon
  About such a moon, you see.

Then there's a harvest moon
  Large and gold and free
And then a lover's moon
  On the banks of the old Swanee.

On every land and every sea
  It seems there's a moon to shine
But give me the mountains of Tennessee
  Where we make our own moonshine.

JACK DANIEL'S

Up a little hollow
   Down yonder in the hills
Forty miles from nowhere
   Among the whippoorwills.

Way back in the ridges
   All out of touch with time
Who could make a product
   To vie with any line?

Who could still a whiskey,
   Still it smooth and fine
To please a choosy palate
   And taste as chaste as mine?

Who could reach perfection
   Where cities fail to glow?
Please don't misjudge, my friend,
   Simple skills that hillfolk know.

Sip and see.

The Old Market Place

And the Old Hardsell

IT'S BEEN SO LONG

It's been so long, so many years
My eyes are blinded by the tears.

She was so young and fair and sweet
When that rascal she chanced to meet.

He told her forty million lies
And stole her right before my eyes.

Now she lives in a castle grand
On ten-thousand acres of land.

And that scoundrel dark and dank
Has twenty millions in the bank.

It pains my heart just to think,
Excuse me while I buy a drink.

WINTER AND SPRING

I'm getting old and feeble
   My bones are full of gout
My mind is now forgetful
   And full of dreadful doubt.

My hand is not so quick
   My step is not so spry,
Still my heart doth flutter
   When girls go prancing by.

I wouldn't mind being poor
if it wasn't for being so short of cash.

The dread of the job
is the worst part.

Keep your nose to the grindstone
And you'll surely wear it out.

This is the gate to nowhere
And the gate to everywhere.

SIMPLE FACTS

I can read, rite and cipher;
    I ain't nobody's fool,
And do multiplication
    Though I've never been to school.

I know that in the morning
    The rooster crows at five
Andya gotta keep a scratchin'
    If you wanna stay alive.

MR. TOM

He set by his word
    A great deal of store,
Gave it but kept it
    No matter the chore.

So to his neighbors
    And his friends untold
His word has become
    More precious than gold.

LITTLE GIRLS

Little girls
   Make lots of noise
To attract
   Little boys.

LEARNING

Learn to creep
    Before you walk
Learn to think
    Before you talk.

Learn to look
    Before you jump
Learn to stop
    Before you bump.

Learn to walk
    Before you fly
Learn to live
    Before you die.

TRUTH

Tell your tales
    So tall and high
But truth is bigger
    Than any lie

For who could dream
    Or by any act
Find deeds so great
    As actual fact.

GONE FISHIN'

Gone fishin'
Gone huntin'
Gone to have me some fun
Gonna catch me a biggun'
Gonna loaf in the sun,
Whoever cares if the work's never done?
Or the money's never made?
I'll be restin' in the mellow summer shade
Restin' and dreamin' while the stream rolls on
I may never get rich but I'll get along.

MY PAPPY

My Pappy says life wasn't meant
    To rush and hurry through
But to love and laugh and be content
    And to think of folks like YOU.

PAPPY'S BOY

I was raised in a log cabin
    And suckled on a jug o' corn,
I started chewing tobacco
    On the day that I was born.

I ain't ascared of the Martins
    And I've killed a thousand Coys
And raising hell in general
    Is the chiefest of my joys.

I never have time for playing
    And to work I just ain't able
But when a meal is ready
    I'm always at the table.

Money never worries me
    And troubles I have none
I'm just a lad from Tennessee
    And full of hell and fun.

A LITTLE TIN BOX

I have a little tin box
  So precious and so dear
Whose value daily increases
  Year after year.

A faded old letter
  And a wisp of her hair
And a wilted red rose
  Are hidden in there.

I view it with sadness
  But why should I sigh
She went off and married
  A mighty fine guy.

LITTLE PATH

A little path goes winding
  Through the field, across the hill
When I was a lad I walked it
  And I can see it still.

I drove the cows around it
  And saw many wondrous sights;
The clouds overhead a sailing
  The meadow larks in flights.

When evening sun was setting
  In the land beyond the hills
I often dreamed of riches
  And listened to whippoorwills.

When summer years rolled by
  And I had older grown
I met a wondrous girl
  And sometimes walked her home.

Oh, little path a-winding
  Through the field, across the hill
To so many wondrous places
  I can see them still.

RECLUSE

I'll build me a castle
    High on a hill,
With a few houn dogs
    And a copper still.

I'll live my life
    In my own free way
And you won't find m
    'Til Judgement Day

CAREFREE

Sing a heigh ho and a heighdy ho
It's hard to believe how little I know;
How little I know, how little I care
I'm as happy as a millionaire.

DECISIONS

Life is filled with many turns
   Which one shall I take,
One to the poorhouse, one to wealth
   Which will make or break?

One to happiness, one to pain
   One to wealth and fame,
How should I know which one to take
   Neither has a name.

MONKEY SHINES

Man used to be a monkey
    A settin' in the trees
A chatterin' at the bluejays,
    A scratchin' at his fleas.

Then along came Mister Darwin
    And invented evolution,
Caused the downfall of monkey
    And all of this commotion.

They say man is very noble
    He can stew, worry and fret,
But I've never seen a monkey
    Up to his ears in debt.

Now I very often wonder
    Would I really better be
A happy lit'l ole monkey
    A settin' in a tree?

AUNT OMA

"Never find fault with what's been done.
Unless you was the one who done it."

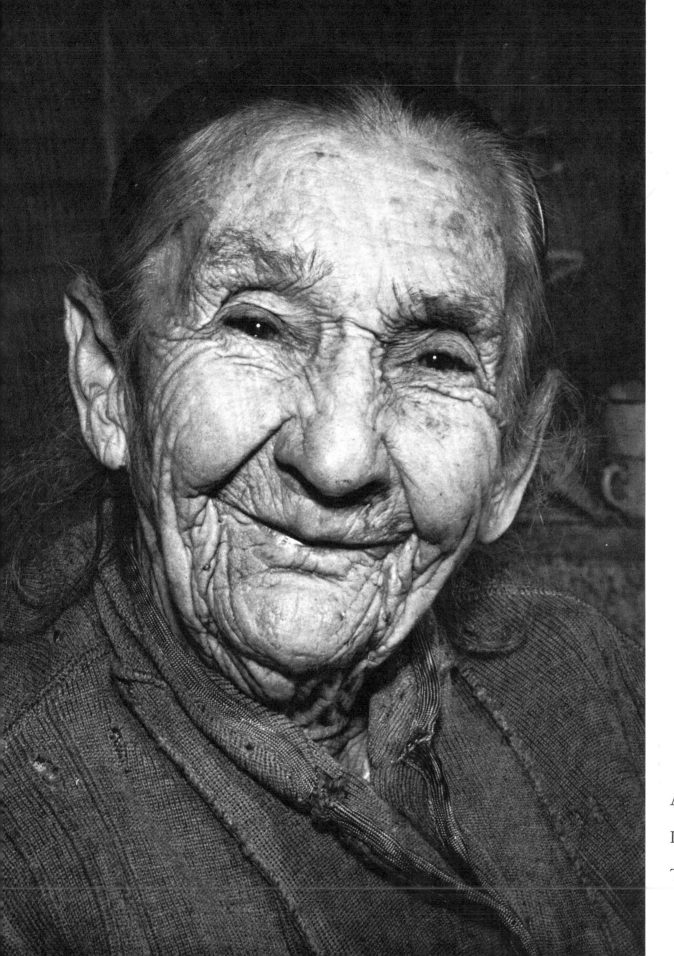

AUNT TILDA

In her heart there glowed a fire
   That filled her eyes with radiant light
Though unlearned and poor she was
   She lived with all her might.

PEOPLE IN THE EARLY DAYS

People in the early days
Had such quaint and ancient ways;
They'd hardly ever take a bath
Or follow in the beaten path.

They fought to win the wild, wild West
And every man done his best
To clear the land and make it free
And safe to live for you and me.

From ignorance they emigrated
And then became educated,
And then before they realized
Courtly, proud and civilized.

Thanks to all the things they done,
Thanks to each and everyone,
You and me can take a bath
And follow in the beaten path.

A LITTLE RHYME

Years go flitting swiftly by
  On enchanted wings of time;
Born one morn, the next to die,
  Life is but a little rhyme.

A little rhyme repeated
  A hundred million times,
A hundred million people
  A hundred million rhymes.

Each rhyme a little different,
  Yet every rhyme the same;
A hundred million people
  Though each a different name.

No matter how you slice 'em,
  The people or the years
All keep swiftly flitting by
  Like countless falling tears.

DEAR MAW

At last I've settled in this big town
With a tie and collar and a suit of brown,
Just me and myself all by ourselves
And a pair of shoes size number twelves.

And if you would ever see a sight
You should see me a steppin' out at night
With a chaw of terbacker and a big segar
And a Stetson hat and a new Ford car.

I'm a regular city feller sure as crows;
Yes, me dressed up in my new store clothes,
And you'll travel far before you'll see
As handsome a lad as hill-billy me.

THE GENERAL STORE

We all used to sit around the old gen'rl store
But we don't sit around no more
For the days are gone and the store is gone
And a supermarket ain't no store.

RELIGION

We went to meetin' in our shirtsleeves
    Got baptised in the creek
And brought the preacher home for dinner
    Every other week.

THE MEETIN' HOUSE

There was a little old meetin' house
    Where we all used to gather 'round
Just to listen to the preacher preach
    And hear him the mighty truths expound.

There he told us of a hell of fire
    And of a Heaven bright with gold,
And of friends who were waiting there
    When from life we release our hold.

He told of rewards for those who love
    And of punishments for those who hate,
'Twas a narrow road to the home above
    And few could enter that golden gate.

The mourners wailed, the women shouted
    As we sang the hymns of love and praise,
That the preacher was right we never doubted
    In those our childhood go-to-meetin' days.

We shook with awe as he waved his arms
    His voice could be heard a mile away
As he tried to save us from those harms
    That come to sinners on Judgement Day.

What is to be will be.
What ain't to be might happen.

SALLY

By a smoky fire
    On a lonely night
She strums her guitar
    Soft and sweet
And in her dreams
    She wanders far
To find the Prince
    She longs to meet.

SINGLE MAN

Spin your yarns
    Tell your tales
Lie your lies
    Drink your ales.

Spend your dough
    Live it up
Life was meant
    For to sup.

Sing your song
    Play your tune
Love the girls
    Come honeymoon.

GIRLS

They are mighty nice
    When you really need them
But don't fool around with girls
    If you want to keep your freedom.

HOW

Girl's smile
  Sweet and gay
Steal boy's
  Heart away.

Bells ring
  Loud and clear
Hearts sing
  Love is dear.

Gold ring
  For her hand
Heart bound
  Like iron band.

That's how
  She gets man
And how
  Life began.

WORLD

In days of old
    In days gone by
When I was young
    And strong and spry
The world was big
    And eager I
Would conquer world
    And lay it by.
Now world so small
    How can it be
That you have got
    The best of me?

MILKING TIME

Up the hill, down the hill
   A cow goes to water
Running round the pasture
   Looking for the fodder.

Up the creek, down the creek
   A lad goes a walking
Looking for Old Bossy
   Evening shadows falling.

Homeward bound, homeward bound
   Whippoorwills a calling
Me and Old Bossy
   Darkness is a falling.

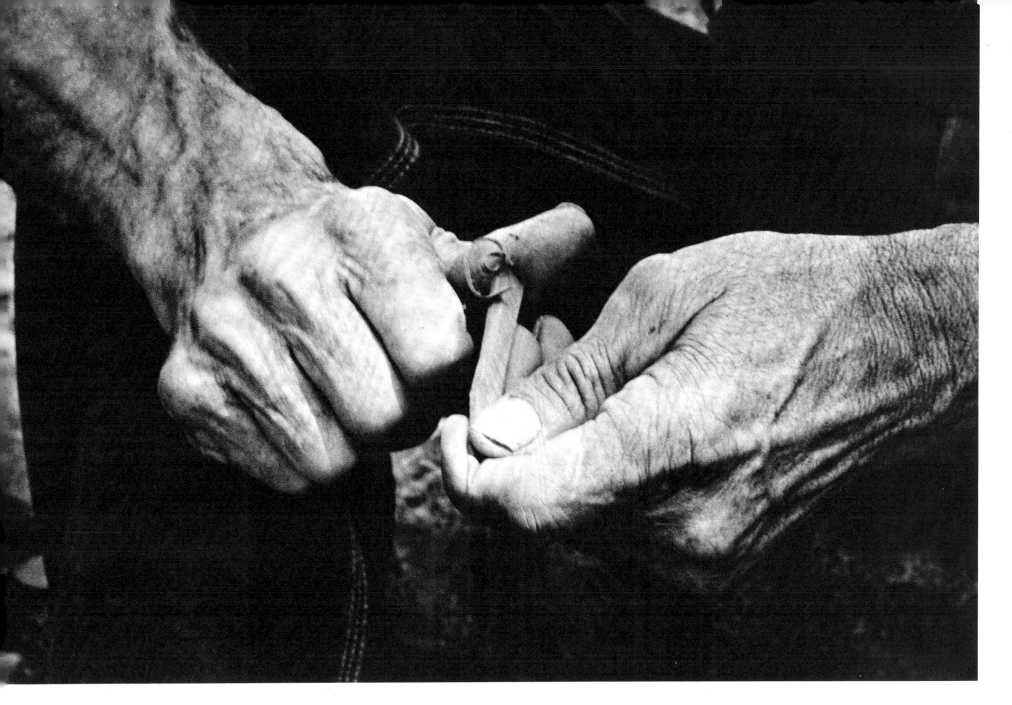

COME SIT WITH ME

Come sit with me when you're lonely,
Come sit with me when you're blue;
And tell me all your troubles
And I'll tell mine to you.

We'll add them all together
And we'll heap them in a pile;
When we've cast them all aside
We'll laugh and joke awhile.

FAR IS FAR

How deep and still the waters run
    How soft and pure the west winds blow
How sweet is life to a mountain boy
    How far can dreams and bullets go?